To

_____

On the occasion of

_____

From

_____

Date

Our Baby
The first five years

A LION BOOK

Tring · Batavia · Sydney

Published by
Lion Publishing plc
Icknield Way, Tring, Herts, England
ISBN 0 7459 1119 6
Lion Publishing Corporation
1705 Hubbard Avenue, Batavia, Illinois 60510, USA
ISBN 0 7459 1119 6
Albatross Books Pty Ltd
PO Box 320, Sutherland, NSW 2232, Australia
ISBN 0 86760 689 4

Compiled by Marion Stroud

First edition 1986
Reprinted 1987, 1988

Acknowledgments
Colour artwork and cover illustration by Chris Barker
Pencil drawings by Pamela Venus

Bible quotations from Good News Bible, copyright 1966, 1971 and 1976 American Bible
Society, published by Bible Societies/Collins

Extracts from *The Alternative Service Book 1980* are reproduced by permission of the
Central Board of Finance; extract from *The Book of Common Prayer* is reproduced by
permission of The Church Pension Fund; extracts from *The Methodist Service Book* by
permission of the Methodist Conference

Other copyright material as follows: Hanna Ahrens, *Who'd Be a Mum?*, Lion Publishing,
1982, pages 32, 42; Mary Batchelor, *Bringing up a Family*, Lion Publishing, 1981, page 30;
Henry Brandt, *Living Quotations for Christians*, ed. Sherwood E. Wirt and Kersten
Beckstrom, Hodder and Stoughton Ltd, 1975, page 33; Helen Good Brenneman,
Meditations for a New Mother, Herald Press, 1953, page 14; Brother John Charles,
Contemporary Parish Prayers, Mowbrays Publishing Division, page 8; Frank Colquhoun,
Family Prayers, Triangle Books/SPCK, 1984, pages 33, 45; Llewellyn Cumings, *Family
Prayers*, Triangle Books/SPCK, 1984, page 37; Paula D'Arcy, *Song for Sarah*, Lion
Publishing, 1981, page 10; James Dobson, *Discipline While You Can*, Kingsway Publications,
1978 and *The Strong-Willed Child*, Tyndale House Publishers, 1978, pages 18, 38; James
Dobson, *Hide or Seek*, Hodder and Stoughton Ltd, 1982, page 40; Jack Dominian, *Marriage,
Faith and Love*, Darton, Longman and Todd Ltd, 1981, pages 8, 17, 26, 40; Elizabeth
Goudge, *The Joy of the Snow*, Hodder and Stoughton Ltd, page 18; Roger Forster, *We Believe
in Marriage*, Marshall Pickering, page 10; Pat King, *How Do You Find the Time?*,
Marshall Pickering, 1982, page 22; Laurie Lee, *I Can't Stay Long*, Andre Deutsch Ltd, pages
10, 12, 26; A.A. Milne, *Now We Are Six*, Methuen Children's Books, McClelland and Stewart
Ltd (Toronto), E.P. Dutton (New York), page 44; Carolyn Nystrom, *Fostering No Illusions*,
Moody Press, 1979, pages 12, 29; David Porter, *Through the Eyes of A Child*, Lion
Publishing, 1984, page 36; Edith Schaeffer, *What is a Family?*, Hodder and Stoughton Ltd,
1975, pages 19, 28, 32; Katharine Short, *A Book for Mums*, Lion Publishing, 1981, pages 38,
45; Jean Watson, *Happy Families*, Hodder and Stoughton Ltd, 1983, pages 12, 16, 18, 22, 28,
38, 42

Every effort has been made to trace and contact copyright owners. If there are any
inadvertent omissions in the acknowledgments, we apologize to those concerned

British Library Cataloguing in Publication Data
Our baby : the first five years.
   1. Children——Quotations, Maxims, etc.
   2. Infants——Quotations, Maxims, etc.
   I. Stroud, Marion
   305.2'3   PN6084.C5
   ISBN 0 7459 1119 6

Library of Congress Cataloging-in-Publication Data
Our baby: the first five years
   A Lion book.
   1. Parents——Prayer-books and devotions——English.
   I. Stroud, Marion.
   BV4845.096   1986   242'.64   86-20925
   ISBN 0 7459 1119 6

Printed and bound in Italy

Introduction

A child is born! So many dreams, hopes and plans are wrapped around this tiny person. A new life has begun . . . and your life will never be the same again.

Every child is an individual in his own right, and so are his mother and father. As your baby moves from the total dependence of the new-born to the budding independence of the first days of school, you will learn more about love, laughter, anxiety, frustration and just plain tiredness than you ever dreamed existed! For people learn to be parents as they go along. You do not receive a diploma on parentcraft and a baby in the same graduation ceremony! Together you must learn to be a family . . . to love, to give and to forgive. In the early years the giving may seem to flow mostly one way. But those first five years establish the foundations of your future life together. Beginnings are important.

This book gives you the opportunity to record those beginnings. But more than that, it draws on the experience of other parents, a variety of prayers to make your own, and the age-old wisdom of the Bible, to help and encourage you as you set out on the adventure of a lifetime together.

Roots

'God put within us the need to belong, to be loved, accepted, protected and valued. He then designed the family to meet those needs. Within the family, children receive love and care, and in their turn learn to love and care for others.' *MARION STROUD*

'It is in the home that children experience their first relationship of love. Every child forms a bond early in the first year of life and within that bond learns to feel acknowledged, wanted and appreciated . . . Just as all of us receive the gifts of loving because God first loved us, so children receive the capacity to love through their experience of their parents.'

JACK DOMINIAN

'Father of all, accept our thanks
for the joys of family life.
Help us to live so that we may strengthen
and enrich the life of the family.
Help us to build with you the kind
of family which welcomes the stranger,
the lonely and the needy.
Teach us through this small family to
love the family of all mankind and
to realize our part in it.'

Family Tree

Great Grandmother _____

              Grandmother _____

Great Grandfather _____

                         Mother _____

Great Grandmother _____

              Grandfather _____

Great Grandfather _____

                         Name _____

Great Grandmother _____

              Grandmother _____

Great Grandfather _____

                         Father _____

Great Grandmother _____

              Grandfather _____

Great Grandfather _____

A Child is Born

'Ten fingers, ten toes, little you. Perfect you. Watching you stretch your way into this world was the fullest joy I've ever known. Complete. No happiness in my life has ever been that true. I'll carry your first cry with me wherever I go.'
PAULA D'ARCY

'Here she is then, my daughter, here, alive, the one I must possess and guard. A year ago this space was empty, not even a hope of her was in it. Now she's here, brand new, with our name upon her . . .'
LAURIE LEE

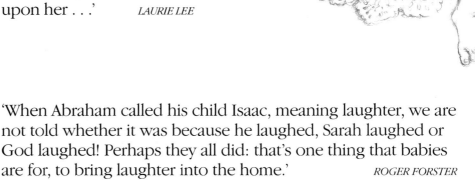

'When Abraham called his child Isaac, meaning laughter, we are not told whether it was because he laughed, Sarah laughed or God laughed! Perhaps they all did: that's one thing that babies are for, to bring laughter into the home.'
ROGER FORSTER

'God is the creator of all things and by the birth of children he gives parents a share in the work and joy of creation.'

THE ALTERNATIVE SERVICE BOOK 1980

Details of Birth

Time	Date
Place	
Weight	Length
Eyes	
Hair	

'God our Father, maker of all that is living, we praise you for the wonder and joy of creation. We thank you from our hearts for the life of this child, for a safe delivery, and for the privilege of parenthood. Accept our thanks and praise through Jesus Christ our Lord. Amen.'

Laying Foundations

'Thank you God for a tiny baby to hold — and this time of
quiet while he eats. His breath is light, skin soft. Tiny fingers
curl confidently round mine. A little foot thumps persistently
against my leg. How joyful he is to be nourished. His whole
body reacts with pleasure. And you are feeding me, too —
feeding me with his love — and yours.'   *CAROLYN NYSTROM*

'It is little more than a month since I was handed this living
heap of expectations, and I can feel nothing but simple awe.'

LAURIE LEE

'Our babies will know whether they can trust us or not, though
it will be a long time before they actually understand this. If we
learn to interpret their movements, sounds and facial
expressions and meet their needs promptly, calmly and
lovingly, we are laying good foundations for building
personalities capable of trusting others.'   *JEAN WATSON*

First Photographs

'Heavenly Father, you have blessed us with the gift of children and trusted them to our care. Give us the understanding and patience we need to bring them up, that we may lead them in the way of Christ and teach them to love whatever is just and true and good, for the glory of your name.'

Bless this Child

'Our wiggly little bundle came at Christmas time, reminding us in a special way that babies are remarkable gifts . . . Scarcely aware of anything beyond himself and his needs, he came to us with an amazing capacity for love, a love which developed and matured as he was loved by other people and learned about the love of God. And most significant of all, this gift was created by God himself, in his own image and for his own glory. Ours for today, he is God's for eternity.'

HELEN GOOD BRENNEMAN

'I asked God for this child, and he gave me what I asked for. So I am dedicating him to the Lord . . .'

HANNAH, AFTER THE BIRTH OF SAMUEL

Baby's Dedication or Christening

Date _____

Time _____

Place _____

Godparents _____

'Some people brought children to Jesus for him to place his hands on them but his disciples scolded the people. When Jesus noticed this he was angry and said to his disciples, "Let the children come to me and do not stop them, because the Kingdom of God belongs to such as these . . ." Then he took the children in his arms, placed his hands on each of them, and blessed them.'

JESUS' WORDS IN MARK'S GOSPEL, CHAPTER 10

Photograph

'The Lord bless you and watch over you,
the Lord make his face to shine upon you
and be gracious to you.
The Lord look kindly on you and give you peace;
and the blessing of God almighty,
the Father, the Son, and the Holy Spirit,
be among you and remain with you always.
Amen.'

15

Milestones

'When their children are small, mothers are prone to worry unnecessarily about relatively unimportant things . . . When you are worried about something to do with your child's progress or lack of it, ask yourself "Will this be a problem at twenty-one?" If the answer is "No" then relax and let things take their course.'

JEAN WATSON

I first smiled

Slept through the night

Laughed

Took solid food

Cut my first tooth

Sat up alone

Crawled

Spoke my first word

Stood alone

Walked

Childhood Illnesses

_____

_____

_____

_____

_____

'These are the years when the child is coping with the first
steps of intellectual growth and needs to be stimulated with
language, objects, toys and games . . . but above all these are
the years when the parents provide a framework for reliable
emotional growth.'

JACK DOMINIAN

*'God our Father, we do not understand pain and suffering, but we know
that you are with us in the bad times as well as the good. Help us to care for
this growing child and to learn to trust in your love.'*

Vaccination Record

on

on

on

on

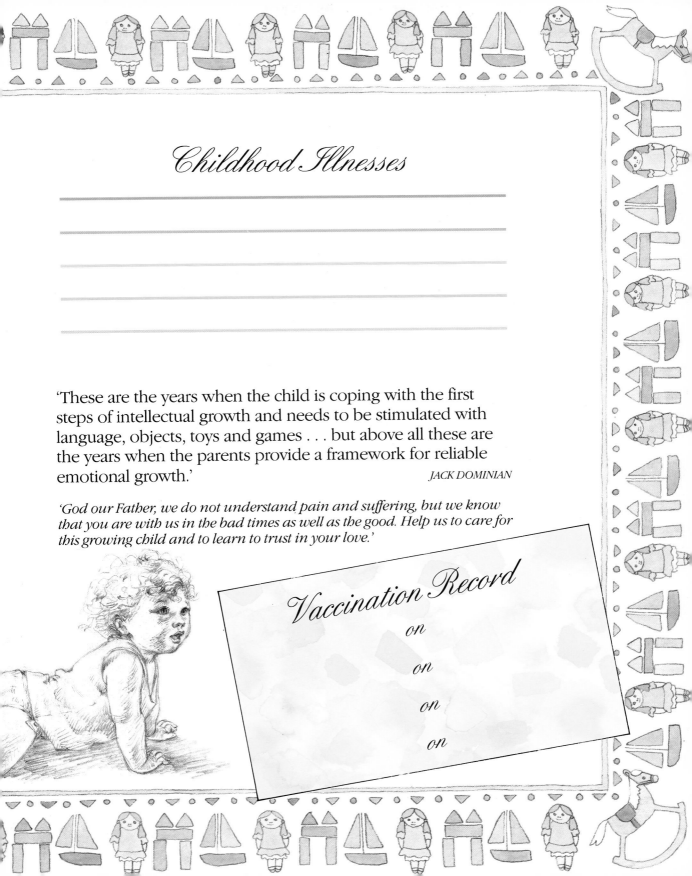

Learning to Love

'My first memory is concerned with raspberries . . . I was standing on a pathway in a forest and on either side of me towered green trees. I looked at them with awe. The pathway stretched before me straight as a ruler, the trees converging to a mysterious vanishing point. My ambulatory powers at that period were those of a very ancient crone. One swayed on the feet, balanced precariously, then gathered courage and staggered forward. But I was not afraid either of my own unbalanced state nor of the towering raspberry canes on either side, nor of the mysterious vanishing point, because ahead of me on the path was my father picking the raspberries.'

ELIZABETH GOUDGE

'A relationship that is characterized by genuine love and affection is likely to be a healthy one . . .'

JAMES DOBSON

'Our children must learn to trust a human being or they will not be able to understand what trusting God means, let alone do it. There are many people who cannot really trust God, because their early experiences of people taught them to be wary and tense.'

JEAN WATSON

18

'Teaching takes place by example, every minute of every day by whoever is with that baby — hour after hour, day after day, month after month.'

EDITH SCHAEFFER

'O God our Father, we thank you for our children; and we ask that we may so show our love and thankfulness that the example of our lives and teaching may guide them in the way of righteousness and love, through Jesus Christ our Lord. Amen.'

Baby's First Birthday

Date

Guests

Presents

Photographs

21

The Joys of Family Life

'This morning two-year-old Patrick said to me, "I want to hold your hand at the beach." No one had to say "you'll regret it if you don't go," for I had learned. We went, the two of us, and overturned rocks, awakened sleepy crabs, peeked into tide pools and fed bread to the gulls. The work waited.'   *PAT KING*

'It is very important for children to feel that their parents actually enjoy playing with them, talking and listening to them. We can start assuring them along these lines very early on in their lives . . . Make sure that some time is given each day to playing or romping at the child's level . . . on the floor!'

JEAN WATSON

'Each day comes just once in a lifetime — today you are creating tomorrow's memories. Invest in positive memories for childhood memories shape the person of the future.'

MARION STROUD

'O God, your generous love surrounds us,
and everything we enjoy comes from you.'

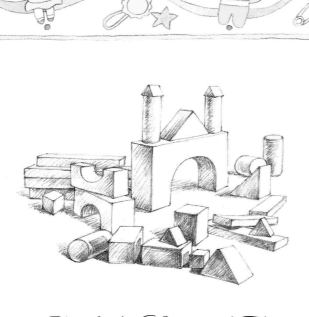

Baby's Special Things

Toys

Lullabies

Books

Food

Songs

Stories

Outings

This is Me

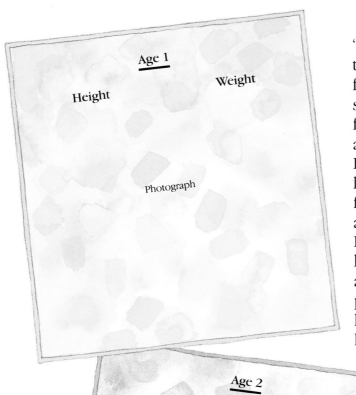

Age 1

Height

Weight

Photograph

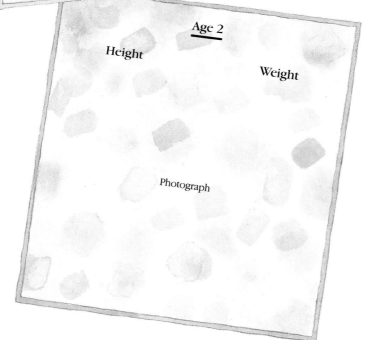

Age 2

Height

Weight

Photograph

'It is quite possible to agree in theory that our children are gifts from God, and then to wish for something other than he gives us, as far as sex, basic personality, appearance or gifts are concerned. Each one of us has the need to be loved and accepted for what we are, from the cradle onwards — so let's accept God's gift to us with joy. Every child is created by God to fill his special place within our hearts and home. He brings with him a particular opportunity for loving and learning that no dream child, however perfect, could provide.'

MARION STROUD

<u>Age 3</u>

Height   Weight

Photograph

<u>Age 4</u>

Height   Weight

Photograph

<u>Age 5</u>

Height   Weight

Photograph

'Children are a gift from the Lord:
they are a real blessing.'

FROM PSALM 127

Look! I can . . .

'She is here for good, her life stretching before us, twenty odd years wrapped up in that bundle; she will grow, learn to totter, to run in the garden, run back, and call this place home.'

LAURIE LEE

'The young child wants to feed itself, learn how to dress, to run about and to do things. All this is achieved by trial and error and with the active assistance of mother.'

JACK DOMINIAN

When I was ____
I learned to climb
the stairs

I learned to walk
when I was ____

When I was ____
I could use the potty

I learned to feed myself
when I was ____

*I first slept in a bed
when I was____*

*When I was____
I could count up to 10*

*I learned to dress myself
when I was____*

*I stayed dry at night
when I was____*

*I learned to swim
when I was____*

*When I was____
I learned to write

my name*

*'God our Father, in giving us this child you
have shown us your love. Help us to be
trustworthy parents. Make us patient and
understanding, that our child may always
be sure of our love and grow up to be
happy and responsible; through Jesus
Christ our Lord. Amen.'*

27

One Step at a Time

'Children's questions must be taken seriously at the ages of two and three, or they won't be continuing to ask you at twelve and twenty-three. The importance of being given answers, and being treated as a significant human being, begins as soon as answers are asked for . . . One never knows which answer, which explanation, which attitude . . . is going to be *the* important one.'

EDITH SCHAEFFER

'Informal teaching at home can happen at meal times, on walks, at bedtime, in the bath, while playing and working — the facts of God's presence, provision, interest, relevance and help can spill out of us quite naturally provided we truly believe them . . . Our children can begin to see that all things come from God, and all are dependent on him.'

JEAN WATSON

'Where does your lap go when you stand up?'

'Where did my baby sister come from?'

'Who made God?'

'Why did my rabbit die?'

'Why doesn't the sky fall down?'

28

'Lord Jesus,
"Lord, teach us to pray" your disciples once said. And you lovingly taught
them. Now I'm asked to teach my children to pray . . . Let them think of you
as someone who knows them personally and loves them dearly — not a
frightening, mysterious, all-seeing eye. Help them not to regard prayer as a
magic wishing-well. Let them understand that they can talk to you without
following any set form or pattern, for you are their friend as well as their
God. Let my prayers be good examples to my children. And thank you for
all that I am learning as you teach our little children — and me, your older
child — to pray.'

One of the Family

'Although he or she is yours, your baby belongs to the bigger family of grandparents, aunts, uncles and cousins. Christians belong to a family that's bigger than their own blood relations. The church is the family of those whose father is God himself. You will want to introduce your baby quite soon into the fellowship of your own local church.'

MARY BATCHELOR

I began attending church on

The hymn or song I like best is

The Bible story I like best is

'God our Father, bless our home and family and teach us to live together in your love. Help us to bring up our children in the light of your truth so that by our care and example they will grow up to love and follow you.'

A Child's Prayer

Thank you for the world so sweet
Thank you for the food we eat
Thank you for the birds that sing
Thank you, God, for everything!

31

Right and Wrong

'Michael is having one of his "No" days. On days like this I forget that tantrums are only tantrums . . . I read out a story about Mickey Mouse going to the moon.

"Why do you need space suits and helmets?" asks Michael.

"Because there's no oxygen on the moon," I answer.

"No," says Michael.

"Right, now get into the bath."

"No."

"Then I'll have to do my trick on my own!"

"What trick?"

"The one with the macaroni and shampoo."

"Can I come too?"

"Yes."

We make bubbles in the bath tub, mountains of bubbles which slowly roll over the edge of the tub. At last Michael's defiance evaporates in sheer delight. While I rinse his back and rub him dry with a warm towel, he hugs me with still dripping arms and says, "I do love you so much!"

HANNA AHRENS

'Children should learn very early . . . that mistakes are made . . . and we all fall into times of misbehaving . . . Apologies should be made to small children by parents. The understanding of what an apology is, and what forgiveness is, should be a two-way street, from the very beginning.'

EDITH SCHAEFFER

'To discipline a child is not to punish him for stepping out of line, but to teach that child the way he ought to go. Discipline therefore includes everything that you do in order to help the children learn.'

HENRY. R. BRANDT

'Teach a child how he should live, and he will remember it all his life.'

FROM THE BOOK OF PROVERBS, CHAPTER 22

'God of love, we pray for our children as they grow up in our family circle. Give us understanding of their needs and show us how best we can help them as they face their problems and prepare for life in the wider world outside. Help us to establish a relationship of trust between them and ourselves, and to make our home a place where at all times they may find love and security.'

33

My Holidays

Photographs

Photographs

My Friends

'Children . . . don't ask questions of each other. There's an extraordinary acceptance, a willingness to strike up friendly chatter at a moment's notice. They have one or two special friends — and they talk about them a lot and quote things they've said. Oddly, when they're together, there are quite often tears and tantrums, quivering lips and stormy quarrels, generally short-lived . . . It's like the best kind of adult friendship — tolerant, unassuming, able to weather the occasional argument.'

DAVID PORTER

'Lord Jesus, thank you for being our friend and for enriching our lives with so many gifts of your love. Thank you too for human friends and for all that they mean to us. We thank you especially for those who have helped us and stood by us in difficult times. Help us, who have received so much, to give true friendship to others in your name and for your sake.'

37

Letting Go

'In the beginning we have to do virtually everything for our babies but gradually our role will change. Instead of doing things for our children we will more and more enable them to manage their own affairs. But total freedom will not be granted until they are, or ought to be, ready for it.'

JEAN WATSON

'Our children need guide-lines. Freedom isn't flying off in all directions at once. It's learning to deal with the risks, to change what can be changed, to accept what can't, to fit in with other people, to be the best that we can be.'

KATH SHORT

'The parental purpose should be to grant increasing freedom and responsibility year by year, so that when children get beyond adult control, they will no longer need it.'

JAMES DOBSON

'Thank you, Father, for letting me care for
this child, for the joy of watching him grow.
Help me to provide the warmth, the love,
and the security he needs now, so that
when he stands alone, he will do so with
courage and with confidence.'

The Big, Wide World

'Separation is a delicate matter and needs to take place at a graduated pace. Gradually the child can cope with physical aloneness without the panic of isolation and loneliness.'

JACK DOMINIAN

'Talk about the exciting things they will soon do in preschool. Try to whet their appetites during the two weeks prior to entry. Take them to visit the teacher at least twice, perhaps on consecutive days . . . Tip off the teacher as to the name of their dog or cat and other familiar topics they can discuss. Let them observe the children in play from the sidelines with you standing nearby. The fourth step brings "plunge-in" day — even if they yell when you leave. Their peers will do the rest.'

JAMES DOBSON

A Child's Prayer
'Thank you, God for my new playgroup.
I want to go again tomorrow.
Goodnight.'

Preschool or Playgroup

Name of preschool or playgroup

Name of teacher

Date started

Date finished

Names of friends

What I like best

The Joy of Learning

'"Michael, what's a bird's nest doing on the bookshelf?"

"You don't understand — I want to keep it for the birds. Then they won't need to build a new one in the spring. I'll put it in the garden, and then I can watch them having baby birds and feeding them."

"Well, that's a nice idea."

Joy, enthusiasm, imagination . . . are more important than keeping things clean and tidy. The nest stays on the shelf.

Meanwhile I've discovered from an expert on mites that each nest contains about a thousand fleas and mites, and that birds are right to build themselves new nests! But how can I explain to Michael what mites are? I only have the vaguest idea myself. They are so small, and Michael is so small, and he only wanted to help the birds . . .'

HANNA AHRENS

'It's very important to establish a good relationship with our children's teachers and to show we're prepared to give as well as take . . . Trusting, backing up and praying for them will help everyone far more than criticizing them, taking too much of their time and seeing them only in relation to our own children, rather than people in their own right with a hard job to do.'

JEAN WATSON

My School

My school is called

My teacher's name is

There are _____ children in my class

My friends are

When I grow up, I want to be

I can write my name

'Thank you, Father, for all the good things you give to us. Thank you for life and health, for families and friends, for food and clothing and for work and play. Thank you for our teachers and for the joy of being able to learn. Help us to understand all that we are taught and to grow up to love and serve you always.'

More Photographs of Me!

Photographs

When I was One,
I had just begun.

When I was Two,
I was nearly new.

When I was Three,
I was hardly Me.

When I was Four,
I was not much more.

When I was Five,
I was just alive.

But now I am Six, I'm as clever as clever.
So I think I'll be six now for ever and ever.
A.A. MILNE

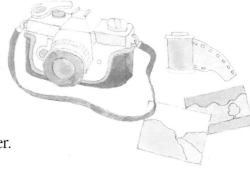

44

'What do I remember, looking back? Beds made, and shopping done? Housework finished and work carried out efficiently? Not a bit of it. I remember the odd unexpected moments . . . moments spent by the pool, instead of hurrying home from school; visits to the local park to see the black sheep with curly horns . . . Time is important.'   *KATH SHORT*

Photographs

'Heavenly Father, how good you are! How wonderful are your works. We praise you for all your gifts, and especially for your gift to us of this dear child.'

45